dabble lab

MAKE MIND-BLOWING MUSIC VIDEOS

Thomas Kingsley Troupe

raintree

a Capstone company — publishers for children

Raintree is an imprint of Capstone Global Library Limited, a company incorporated in England and Wales having its registered office at 264 Banbury Road, Oxford, OX2 7DY – Registered company number: 6695582

www.raintree.co.uk
myorders@raintree.co.uk

Edited by Shelly Lyons
Designed by Sarah Bennett
Original illustrations © Capstone Global Library Limited 2020
Picture research by Morgan Walters
Production by Katy LaVigne
Originated by Capstone Global Library Ltd
Printed and bound in India

978 1 4747 8738 3 (hardback)
978 1 4747 6798 9 (paperback)

British Library Cataloguing in Publication Data
A full catalogue record for this book is available from the British Library.

Acknowledgements
We would like to thank the following for permission to reproduce photographs: All photos by Capstone Studio, Karon Dubke, with the exception of: Shutterstock: ArrowStudio, (girls) Cover, 15; Astarina, (movie action) Cover; Can Yesil, (phone) Cover; Darcraft, (rec) Cover; handini_atmodiwiryo, (books) 11; koonsiri boonnak, top right 4; Lightspring, (stage) 45; mhatzapa, (music notes) 5; mixform design, 16, 21, 40; Natasha Pankina, design element throughout; ONYXprj, (gadgets) 15, 28–29, 44; paniti Alapon, 38; Ramona Kaulitzki, design element throughout; Rolau Elena, design element throughout; Seth Gallmeyer, (notebook) design element; Shorena Tedliashvili, (film strip) design element; silm, design element throughout; Tono Balaguer, bottom 4; Vissay, (poster) 45; Vyacheslav Sakhatsky, (tripod) 11

CONTENTS

Music video magic

What are music videos?

A guitar wails as the lights go up and a band takes the stage. The drumbeat kicks in. The lead singer grabs the microphone. Is this a rock concert? No. It's a music video! Music videos are short films that are used to promote a song. With flashy visuals and dynamic shots, they're designed to get people excited about a song and the band behind the music.

Music video success guide

Be patient Filmmaking is something that needs practice. You won't make a perfect music video the first time, the second time or ever. Practice makes *better*, never perfect.

Plan it out Even though it sounds simple to just show people lip-synching to a song or a band playing instruments, it's a huge help to have a plan in place. Is the video going to tell a story? Will it highlight the band? Will it do a bit of both?

Experiment Try new things, including shooting from different angles. Experiment with black and white or colour. Make your music video stand out by giving it YOUR flavour and something that will complement the band or singer's music.

What you'll need
☆ an idea
☆ a song
☆ a storyboard
☆ talent/band
☆ a video camera/ smartphone/tablet
☆ a location
☆ lights
☆ a microphone
☆ a tripod
☆ editing software

Finding gear

Creating your own music video shouldn't drain your wallet. You can probably find everything you need for your production around the house. Don't put your vision on hold until you can buy the best gear. Lots of great music videos have been made for next to nothing. Use what you have to make music video magic!

Camera ready

Digital cameras

One of the most important tools when making your music video is your camera. Find a digital camera that is simple to use and able to record long clips of video. You'll be taking lots of shots of the musicians, so make sure the camera's memory card has plenty of space on it.

Smartphones & tablets

If you can use a smartphone or a tablet as your camera, you're in luck. Not only are smartphones small and easy to use, many of them have video-editing apps built in. If not, you can always add one. Make sure you ask an adult to help you download the app you need. And don't forget to check that there's enough memory available for all of your video footage.

Lighting

As well as the camera, you'll need light. Use lamps, overhead lights, whatever you can find to brighten up the scene. Natural light works well, too. Keep in mind that sunlight will change throughout the day.

Place your light source out of the camera's range. You don't want to see cords or lights, if possible. Aim the lights at your talent so their faces and instruments are lit up. Try to avoid odd, distracting shadows. Your aim is for viewers to focus on the musicians.

Tripods

A tripod is a great tool that helps keep your shots steady. No need to spend lots of money. You can find inexpensive options out there. Most tripods have adjustable legs and heads that will allow you to change the camera's height.

Tabletop tripods let you place cameras on shelves, tables or anywhere that takes your fancy! If you don't have a tripod, use books or something sturdy to keep your camera in place.

phone tripod →

PRO TIP

Don't feel as though you HAVE to keep your camera locked onto a tripod. Sometimes going "hand held" will give your video a different feel and will allow you to capture things from many angles.

Find that song!

Once you have the important kit, your next job is to find the right song. This is the song that you'll build the music video around.

The type of song you choose will probably drive how the video will look and feel. If it's a slow song, you might use long, mellow shots. Fast, rockin' and up-tempo songs mean you'll probably keep things moving and edit lots of different shots. The big rule? There are (more-or-less) no rules when making a music video!

PRO TIP

If you can, try to use a song that you've created or someone you know has recorded. Songs from popular artists are tricky and can get you in trouble if you don't have permission to use them first!

Idea factory

Coming up with an idea for a music video is one of the best parts. Do you want to film a band playing music? Want to make a mini-film that tells a story based on the song's lyrics? Maybe it should include an arty splash of colour and sound?

Keep in mind that you're doing a low/no-budget video. You probably can't have explosions behind the band or really expensive special effects. Think about what you've got to work with and do your best with what you have. Some of the best music videos are really simple and cheap.

PRO TIP

Need some ideas for your music video? Check out some of the videos other people have made. Just make sure you make YOUR video your own!

Script-tastic!

Writing a script for a music video might seem like a waste of time. But even if your video is just going to be a band playing in the middle of an auditorium, it still helps to have some structure to the shoot. If the video is more like a mini-film, you will definitely want to write out who will say what. You'll also need to write out the action that will take place.

Your script doesn't need to look like a professional Hollywood script. Start with the song's lyrics. Look at the words and decide what you'd like to have happen at each part of the song. If characters will speak in the video, add that to the script, too. Scripts can also be broken down into segments of time.

Script for "Too late"

VERSE ONE	SCENES
☑ Wake up! It's time for school.	I wake up. My surprised face! Close-up: Alarm clock
☐ No PJs, it's time for clothes!	I'm throwing clothes out of my drawers.
☐ Brush my hair and brush my teeth.	Frothy teeth brushing!
☐ Why didn't my alarm ring? It's 9 o'clock, school starts at 8.	Cut away to me shoving books into my school bag.
☐ Oh no! Oh no! I think I'm too late! What will I do today? Oh no!	

PRO TIP

Put check boxes along the side of the song's lyrics. Once you've filmed each part, check off the parts of the song you've captured. You'll know you've got everything when all the boxes are checked.

Storyboard basics

In addition to a script, it's a great idea to create a storyboard. A storyboard is a bit like a comic strip. You can draw in what each shot for the music video might look like. Think of it like a visual checklist of the things you'd like to capture.

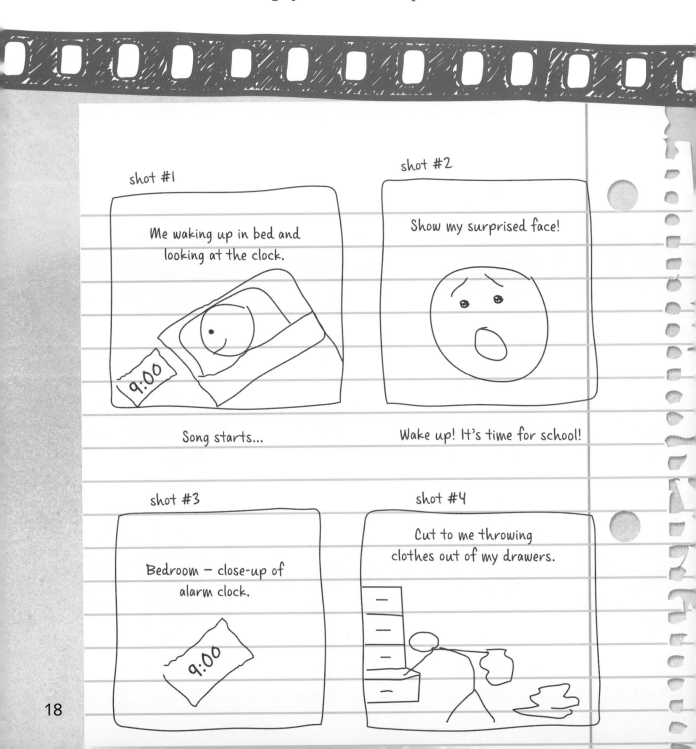

shot #1

Me waking up in bed and looking at the clock.

9:00

Song starts...

shot #2

Show my surprised face!

Wake up! It's time for school!

shot #3

Bedroom – close-up of alarm clock.

9:00

shot #4

Cut to me throwing clothes out of my drawers.

Don't spend a lot of time making each panel in the storyboard perfect. You can draw stick figures and rough sketches to fill in the panels. The important thing is to make sure you draw all the shots that will make up your music video.

shot #5

Cut to bathroom:
Me brushing my teeth.

Brush my hair
and brush my teeth.

shot #6

Shot of me shoving books
into my school bag.

Why didn't my alarm ring? It's
9 o'clock, school starts at 8.

shot #7

I'm freaking out!

shot #8

CHORUS STARTS:
We're all lip-synching
in the garage.

Band together

Most music videos feature the artists and musicians who've created the song. They're basically the stars of the show and should be in the video, if possible.

If the musicians can't be in the video, ask your friends to do some acting. They could stand in and pretend to play instruments. If the music video is more story-based than onstage performance, they could play characters. Your only limit is your imagination!

Filming with friends can be lots of fun!

PRO TIP

Don't have anyone to appear in the video? Film random shots of things happening in your house or local high street. Chances are, when you add the music to it, it'll feel like a music video.

Location, location!

You've got all of your equipment together, your script and storyboard are in great shape and you have people willing to help make the video. Now what? Time to find a location!

Try to find a unique, interesting place for your viewers to look at. Maybe there's a big garage with a lots of old things in it, or a cellar with really funky wallpaper. Avoid using a place that's plain and forgettable. You want people to remember your music video! If the location isn't local, ask an adult to drive you there. The best part about this option? You won't have to carry all of your equipment across town!

PRO TIP

Take time to find the perfect location. You'll need a place with plug sockets and enough room for equipment and props. You'll want the location to be visually interesting, too. Remember – the location will drive the overall look and feel of the video.

Get permission

You've found the perfect location for your shoot. All you need to do is set up and get the camera rolling, right? Wrong! Nothing can shut down a video shoot more quickly than being told you're not allowed to film somewhere.

Make sure you're allowed to film in the location you plan to shoot your music video. Ask permission, even if it's just at a friend's house, your grandma's attic or the local park. Some people are very picky about what happens in their property. There are also locations that will charge a fee for filming there.

And . . . action!

At long last, it's time to shoot your video! Consult your script and storyboard to determine which shot you'd like to film first. Turn on your lights, place your camera on the tripod and ask your talent to move to their places for the first shot.

Let the band or actors know what they need to do for each shot. If they're going to mimic playing music, consider playing that part of the song. Film the same part a few times until you feel like you've got the shots you want.

Let's try again. This time look at the camera.

Awesome! ☺

☑ Wake up!
  It's time for school.

☐ No PJs,
  it's time for clothes!

☐ Brush my hair and
  brush my teeth.

☑ Why didn't my alarm
  ring? It's 9 o'clock,
  school starts at 8.

☑ Oh no! Oh no!
  I think I'm too late!
  What will I do today?
  Oh no!

PRO TIP

There's no rule that says you need to film the scenes in order. As long as you keep track of what you're shooting and what you need, shoot in any order you want!

27

Shot options

To keep your video interesting, you need some variety! Adjust the camera, shoot different things in the room or shoot from different angles. Try some of these camera shots:

Pan and tilt shots – moving the camera from left to right (pan) or moving the camera up or down (tilt)

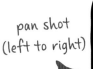

pan shot
(left to right)

tilt shot
(up or down)

PRO TIP

Capture as much as possible when shooting. Don't worry about having too much footage. You can decide what to keep and what to cut later. Having more than you need is better than needing more than you have!

Exterior shot – filming the location where the video is taking place; if you're filming inside a garage, for example, film a bit of the outside of the building; exterior shots help your audience get a clear sense of the location

Close-up – getting up close and personal to the object, place or person you're filming

Zoom – using the built-in zoom feature to move closer to (zoom in) or further away from (zoom out) the person, place or object you're filming; this is sometimes a sliding bar or a button on a digital camera

wide-angle
(pull camera back)

Wide-angle – pulling the camera back so more of the scene is shown

Me waking up and looking at the clock ⇨ shot from the side of the bed

Coverage

While shooting the video, it's a good idea to keep a few things in mind. First, make sure you've got all the shots that were planned in your script and storyboard. Second, make sure you've got enough coverage.

One way to make sure you've got coverage is to shoot the same shot but from another angle. Perhaps start by shooting a close-up of a character getting out of bed. Once you have that shot, pull the camera back or change the angle. Shoot it again from a new position. Now you've got coverage and plenty of options when editing.

Same scene ⇨ shot from above

PRO TIP

Make sure you give your talent and friends breaks from time to time. A video can take a while, so it's good to have snacks and water available. Treat your crew well, and they'll stick around to help!

Cutaways

Giving the audience a break from seeing the same thing for three to four minutes is important. Humans tend to have short attention spans, so between shots of the band, it's sometimes nice to cut away to shots of other things or people.

Your location should give you plenty of ideas. Perhaps film a close-up of a guitar or ukulele. Record something happening outside or even an interesting object in the room. Again, it's all about having options when you edit.

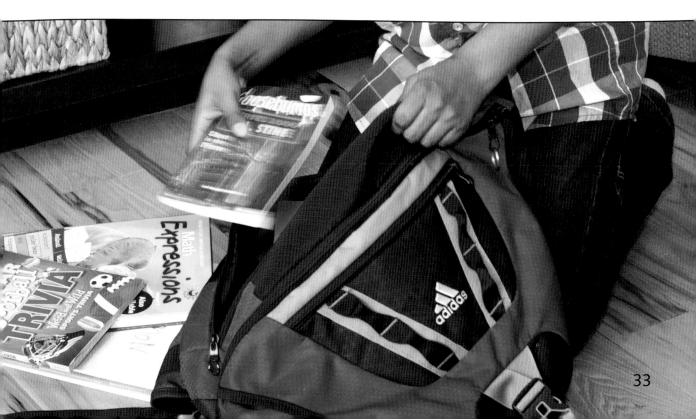

Cutting room

Do you like putting puzzles together? If so, you're going to love editing. When you've finished all the filming and you're satisfied with the shots you've captured, it's time to put the pieces into place. Now is the time to make your music video come to life!

The first step in the editing process is to upload the video you've shot to your editing app/software. Because this is a music video, you'll also need to upload the song. The song is going to be your guide while you're editing.

PRO TIP

Look through your shots and try to number them in the order they should appear. This will help when you arrange the pieces in your music video puzzle.

Rough cut

Play the song while in the editing room to get you started. This will help you visualise the music video. If you need the wide shot of the band for your opening first few seconds, find that footage. Drop the best version of each shot where it belongs during the song, then move to the next piece. Your storyboard and script should help you locate which shot goes where.

When all the shots are in place, you have a "rough cut" of your music video. Congratulations! Now watch the whole thing. Keep in mind that it's going to be clunky. Take notes about areas you'd like to trim and change.

PRO TIP

The rough cut is just that — ROUGH. Don't be discouraged if it doesn't line up perfectly with the lyrics or music. Watching the rough cut is just a first step in the editing process that helps to get everything into position.

Fine-tuning

Now that you've seen the rough version of your video, it's time to fine-tune it. Cut out the parts that don't work. Edit in some of your alternative takes, and keep each shot short and sweet. Remember, viewers will get bored of seeing the same thing for too long.

Oh no! I'm late for school!

If you can, time your edits with the beats in a song. If there's a big drum hit, jump to another shot. If you can edit your video in time with the music, it will seem as though you planned it that way all along!

PRO TIP

Never permanently delete any of your footage! Even if you cut something from the final video, it's a good idea to keep it, just in case you need it later.

Sound and visual effects

The bulk of the sound for your music video will be the song you've chosen. However, there might be places where a character speaks or a sound effect is needed. If so, you can record dialogue or drop a sound clip into the video. Just remember, the song is the star. Be careful not to overdo the effects.

A lot of editing programs allow you to change the colour of the video. Want to make it look old-fashioned? Try changing it to black and white. Some filters can give the video a scratchy, true film look. Experiment! And remember, you can always change it back if you don't like it. If your video is more like a story, consider fading between scenes. It will give the music video a more film-like feel, instead of clunky, rapid cuts.

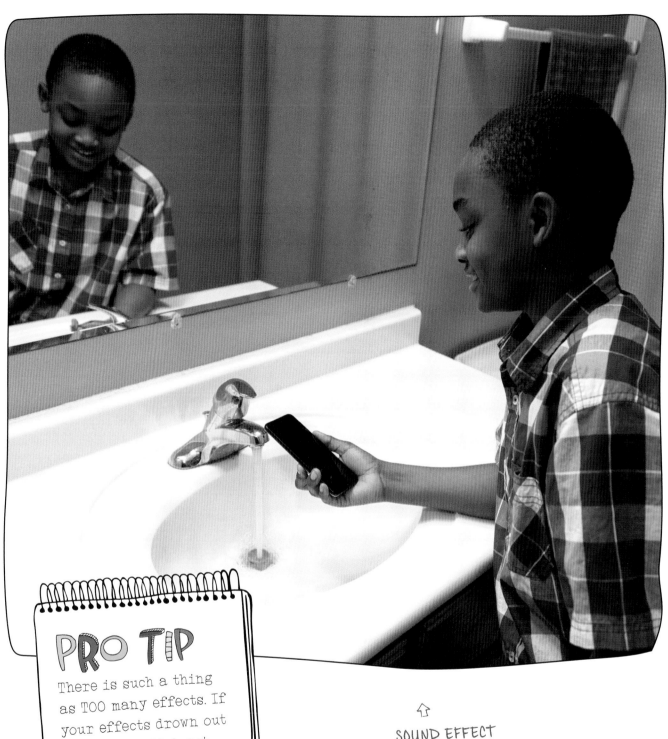

PRO TIP

There is such a thing as TOO many effects. If your effects drown out the song or distract from what's happening on screen, take them out or make another version of the video.

⇧
SOUND EFFECT
Record running water, and then add the sound effect to the toothbrushing clip.

Add credits

Unlike films and documentaries, music videos don't really have credits that scroll at the end. Instead, they tend to put artist information in the lower left corner at the beginning of the video.

> **Example:**
> ARTIST: Noah Gassman
> SONG: "Too late"
> DIRECTOR: Jaden
> CREW: Lydia and Maya

Having credits at the beginning of the video lets viewers know the name of the group and the title of the song. They might love the music and video enough that they'll want to buy the song for themselves!

PRO TIP

Don't forget to thank the people who helped you create the video. Add credits for each of your crew members, too.

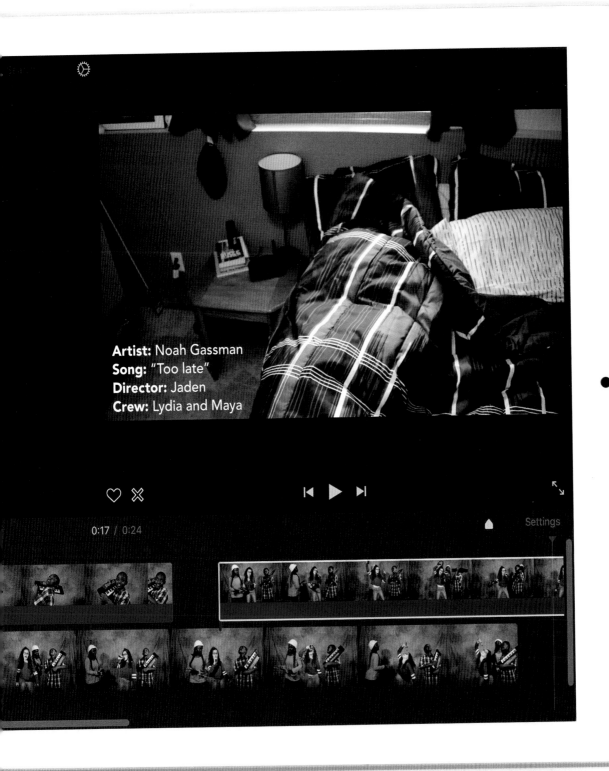

Artist: Noah Gassman
Song: "Too late"
Director: Jaden
Crew: Lydia and Maya

0:17 / 0:24

Settings

Centre stage

Sharing your video

Now it's time to share your video with your soon-to-be fans. Make a big deal about it! Have a premiere night at your house and invite your family to watch it. If your friends have made some videos, too, turn the night into a video showcase. Perhaps you'd like people around the world to watch it? Get permission from all the people in the video first. Then see if your parents/guardians will help you upload it to the internet (YouTube, Vimeo).

That's a wrap!

Now that you've created your first music video, go and make another one. Using what you've learned, you can make something even better than your original. With a new song in your head, you can try some new tricks to bring the music to life. Just keep practising. In no time, you'll have bands begging you to make their next music video!

PRO TIP

If you don't want to use your real name (or other identifying information), make sure you remove it from the video before posting it online. Remember not to upload videos with music you don't have permission to use!

Meet your film instructor

Thomas Kingsley Troupe is an amateur filmmaker who has been making films and videos since he was at secondary school. Thomas has worked in the visual effects department for a handful of Hollywood films and shows. He has also written and directed a number of short films for the 48 Hour Film Fest & Z Fest contests and loves creating funny videos with his own sons at home. Thomas says, "Making films is the BEST. It can be a lot of work, but finishing a film to show to your friends and family is WORTH IT!"

Find out more

Books

Behind the Scenes Film Careers (Behind the Glamour), Danielle S. Hammelef (Raintree, 2018)

Create Your Own Music (Media Genius), Matthew Anniss (Raintree, 2016)

Website

musiclab.chromeexperiments.com/Experiments
Use the Chrome Music Lab to make and share your own songs.

Glossary

app computer application

complement complete or enhance something

coverage amount of footage and different camera angles used to capture a scene

dynamic constantly changing

edit cut and rearrange pieces of film to make a film or TV programme

premiere first public performance of a film, play or work of music or dance

rough cut first version of a film after early editing

scene part of a story, play or film that shows what is happening in one place and time

script story for a play, film or TV programme

segment separate piece of something (such as an interview in a film documentary)

storyboard series of drawings that shows the plot of a TV programme or film

tempo speed or rhythm of a piece of music

Apps and software

Green Screen, by Do Ink – helps users create videos using the green screen effect

iMovie, by Apple – app to help you create your own films

Movie Maker 10, by Microsoft – full filmmaking software for all budding artists

Index